Original title:

Laughter by the Lodgepole

Copyright © 2025 Creative Arts Management OÜ

All rights reserved.

Author: Natalia Harrington

ISBN HARDBACK: 978-1-80567-290-6

ISBN PAPERBACK: 978-1-80567-589-1

Smiles Dancing on the Wind

Giggles flutter through the air,
A chorus of joy beyond compare.
With every twist and every turn,
The softest chuckles start to burn.

Branches sway to silent glee,
As shadows play on you and me.
Nature's jesters, bold and free,
Whisper secrets, wild and breezy.

Tales of Amusement in the Pines

Underneath the pine tree's grace,
Breezes tell a funny space.
Squirrels frolic, tails held high,
In this woodland, spirits fly.

Branches crack with muffled sound,
Every beam of light is crowned.
Pinecones tumble, rolling free,
Creating jokes, just you and me.

Whimsy in the Whisperwood

In the grove where mischief stirs,
The wind plays tricks, a dance of furs.
Leaves are giggling, rustling light,
Tickled softly by the night.

Fireflies sparkle, crafting jokes,
Amusing stories from the oaks.
Whimsy drifts on every breeze,
A playful tune that aims to please.

Cheerful Echoes Through the Trees

Echoes of merriment resound,
In every nook where joy is found.
Frogs are croaking silly rhymes,
Welcoming all to laugh in chimes.

Sunlight pokes through leafy seams,
Igniting hearts with gleeful dreams.
With every rustle, chuckles sigh,
As nature weaves a joyful cry.

The Joyful Embrace of Nature

In the glade where sunlight plays,
Nature winks in merry rays.
Squirrels dance, with tails held high,
While birds insist they can fly by.

Flowers giggle, petals sway,
Breezes whisper, come what may.
A rabbit hops, with quite a flair,
As if it knows no single care.

Delightful Trills in the Thicket

The frogs perform a grand old show,
With croaks that echo to and fro.
A cunning fox joins in the fun,
Sneaking past under the sun.

Birds trill sweet in bright array,
While critters scamper, jesters play.
Leaves chuckle in the gentle breeze,
As nature twirls in lively tease.

Cheerful Antics Beneath the Boughs

Beneath the trees, the shadows dance,
Where every creature takes a chance.
A raccoon slips on his own paw,
And giggles rise, how sweet it thaw!

Chipmunks chase in comical haste,
Checking each nook, nothing goes to waste.
While the sun casts a silly grin,
Nature's fun is where we begin.

A Festival of Light Hearts

In a patch where daisies bloom,
Joy spreads wide, like sweet perfume.
Bouncing beams that tickle the air,
Invite us in to just share.

The sky's a stage, the clouds a play,
As laughter echoes in a way.
Nature's mirth, both wild and free,
Brings forth smiles in jubilee.

Whimsy Wrapped in Nature's Arms

Beneath the branches, giggles flow,
A squirrel juggling nuts in tow.
The brook sings tunes of playful glee,
As daisies share their secret spree.

The shadows twist, a dance of light,
While frogs recite their jokes at night.
A rabbit hops with silly flair,
With tiny shoes, it leaps through air.

The Cheerful Dance of the Spruce

In a patch of green, they shake and sway,
The needles twinkle, come what may.
The breeze brings tales of joy untold,
As sunlight glimmers, bright and bold.

A bear in boots, a sight to see,
Twisting and turning, wild and free.
The critters join in merry jest,
As mother nature throws her fest.

Glee Among the Conifers

Pines whisper secrets, a jolly breeze,
As chipmunks chuckle, climbing trees.
The earth and sky in playful flight,
Share winks of joy, a pure delight.

A woodpecker taps in rhythmic cheer,
While butterflies dance, fluttering near.
With every rustle, a smile's spread,
In this verdant world where fun is bred.

Sunbeams and Snickers Beneath the Boughs

Sunbeams cascade like golden rain,
While whispers of laughter float again.
The thicket jiggles, a lively tease,
As nature giggles among the trees.

A fox in shades, with style so neat,
Tripping on roots, a comical feat.
The mushrooms chuckle, a fungi crew,
Painting the forest in joy anew.

Heartfelt Amusements in the Underbrush

Tiny creatures tumble round,
With giggles soft, in leaps they bound.
A squirrel's leap, a playful chase,
Nature's jest in every space.

A rabbit hops with silly flair,
While owls chuckle from their lair.
The underbrush a stage so grand,
With joy and mischief, hand in hand.

The Frolicsome Spirit of the Wild

In meadows bright, the shadows dance,
The critters plot their wild romance.
Bees buzz by, with buzzing cheer,
As whispers float for all to hear.

A deer prances with grace anew,
While foxes play in shades of blue.
The wild holds secrets, laughter grows,
In every rustle, joy bestows.

Cheerful Whispers in the Evergreen

The trees conspire with laughter light,
Branches swaying in sheer delight.
A woodpecker knocks to call his kin,
While chipmunks scamper, dashing in.

Underneath the towering green,
Cheerful tales are shared, unseen.
Nature's symphony, sounds divine,
Where every moment feels like wine.

Playful Spirits Beneath the Canopy

Beneath the leaves, a secret play,
Where shadows twist and giggles sway.
The breeze carries a merry tune,
With whispers light, from morn to noon.

An ant parade, so bold and grand,
Plays tricks together—oh, so planned!
As sunbeams chase the clouds above,
The forest laughs in purest love.

Cheerfulness Among the Timber

In the shadow of tall trees,
A squirrel juggle nuts with ease,
Beneath the boughs, the giggles reign,
Echoing through the soft terrain.

The woodpecker taps a silly beat,
As rabbits dance on nimble feet,
Even the breeze joins in the fun,
Spreading cheer 'til day is done.

A sleepy bear in a sunny patch,
Dreams of honey and a big, warm hatch,
The sun paints smiles on every face,
In this playful, wild embrace.

With critters singing all around,
Joy blossoms in the forest ground,
Nature chuckles, life's a game,
In the woods, we all feel the same.

Notes of Joy Among the Needles

In the canopy, a chorus sings,
Nuts and berries, delightful things,
A chipmunk slips on a fallen pine,
While frogs croak jokes, feeling fine.

The sunbeams break like playful rays,
As laughter dances through the maze,
Where spiders weave in comic spins,
And playful critters twist and grins.

The branches sway in rhythmic chuckles,
As deer prance by with joyful buckles,
A fox cracks jokes, oh what a sight,
Through the needles, such pure delight.

Every rustle hides a wink,
As birds create the perfect link,
In this green realm, with cheer abound,
Each moment brings a joyful sound.

Nature's Jolly Orchestra

A symphony plays in dawn's glow,
Where critters dance to nature's flow,
The owls hoot in a comic tune,
As rabbits hop beneath the moon.

With a tap from a beaver's tail,
And a bumblebee's buzzing trail,
The chorus of joy fills the air,
Spreading glee everywhere.

When shadows stretch and whispers swell,
The forest shakes with a mirthful yell,
Even the rocks seem to join the spree,
In this jolly jam, wild and free.

With every note, our spirits soar,
Nature's laughter forevermore,
In the heart of the woodland's song,
Together we laugh, where we belong.

Joy in the Whispering Pines

In the pines where the breezes play,
Squirrels scurry through their day,
Acorns drop, and giggles fly,
Underneath the vast, blue sky.

A finch hops and begins to tease,
Filling the air with melodies,
The rustling leaves, a merry sound,
Joy abounds on this sacred ground.

A playful deer prances near,
Winking as if shedding fear,
As shadows dance and sunlight beams,
The laughter flows like gentle streams.

In every nook, a smile waits,
Nature's humor celebrates,
Among the pines, with cheer so bright,
We find our joy in pure delight.

Resounding Joy in the Woodland Nook

Frogs in their coats start a dance,
A squirrel trips up in a prance.
Breezes sing tunes with a twist,
Every shadow has joys to assist.

The brook giggles past ancient trees,
While owls blink softly, at ease.
A rabbit hops high with delight,
Chasing the sun into night.

Under the quilt of green and gold,
Every secret is playfully told.
The pine cones roll with a playful sound,
As chuckles echo all around.

In the heart of this joyful spree,
Nature's humor is wild and free.
With every step, the woods confide,
A hidden laugh in the forest wide.

The Enchantment of Bright Spirits in the Timber

Bumblebees buzz like a merry band,
Tickling flowers with gentle hand.
Acorns fall, a rhythmic tap,
Tree trunks bounce in a joyful clap.

A fox dons a jester's crown,
While critters frolic around the town.
With twinkling eyes and playful flair,
The logs rock softly, a cheerful air.

Chipmunks chatter in silly tones,
While leaves wink, whispering their hones.
Mirrored pools reflect the fun,
Each ripple glimmers under the sun.

As colors blend in a jubilant show,
The spirit of mirth begins to grow.
Through every nook, joy sparkles bright,
An enchantment of spirits ignites the night.

Whispers of Glee Beneath the Forest Sky

Moonlit beams weave through the pines,
Where the laughter of echoes intertwines.
Bushes shake with secrets untold,
While critters spin tales, bold and old.

With fluttering wings and flappy sounds,
A chorus of joy in the leafy grounds.
Acorns roll like chuckles set free,
A playful waltz between you and me.

Jogging streams hum a jovial tune,
Every ripple dances 'neath the moon.
Ferns nod along with a cheeky sway,
While whispers of glee light the way.

In the embrace of stars so bright,
The woods become a stage of delight.
Where every heart finds a reason to sing,
And the forest celebrates everything.

Enchanted Chuckles in the Thicket

Whispers of giggles echo the trees,
Squirrels parade with comical ease,
In hats made of leaves, they prance and twirl,
Nature's jesters in a playful whirl.

The brook sings a tune, so sprightly and bright,
Crickets join in, with all of their might,
Each rock's a stage for the frolicking crew,
While shadows of fun drift softly on cue.

Mushrooms create seats for a laugh and a tear,
Rabbits in costumes, oh what a cheer!
With each little chuckle that dances around,
The woods grow more joyful, so rich and profound.

Around the old stump, the creatures all meet,
With berries for snacks and a tweet for a beat,
Stories of mischief take flight on the breeze,
Where mirth thrives within the enchanted trees.

Jests of the Wilderness

A fox dons a scarf, quite stylish and grand,
He winks to the owl, who can barely withstand,
The puns over brunch on the old mossy log,
While a raccoon snickers, playing the frog.

Chirping and chortling, the critters unite,
In a realm of jubilation, pure and polite,
Where the tallest of pines makes a swaying stage,
And the trees lend their ears to each whimsical page.

A bear rolls in giggles, oh what a sight,
As bees buzz around in their costume delight,
Pollen spreads laughter, so sweet on the breeze,
An uproar of joy, a feast that won't cease.

Through twinkling stars, all our friends gather 'round,
Creating a magic, so wonderfully sound,
The moon hides her face, she cannot contain,
The jests of the wild, an enchanting refrain.

Elation Found in the Woodland

In shadows of branches that sway to and fro,
A symphony chuckles, oh watch how it grows,
With critters galore, and each moment refined,
A tapestry woven with laughter entwined.

The sun winks down on the misfit parade,
A parade of the playful, in sunlight that's made,
With a jig and a jump, the ferns dance in glee,
While ants draft a tale that's as grand as can be.

In patches of wildflowers, bright colors engage,
As friends gather 'round in a whimsical stage,
For every sweet whisper, a story is spun,
With smiles illuminating everyone.

When dusk starts to fall, and shadows conspire,
The laughter ignites like a glowing bonfire,
With all hearts a-flutter, in woodland delight,
Elation abounds, in the soft, tender night.

Smiles Bursting Through the Canopy

Up high in the trees, where the breezes all play,
A chorus of chuckles sets rhythm to sway,
As critters collaborate, each one in the fray,
Creating a symphony brightening the day.

A troupe of raccoons with their cheeks stuffed with food,
Their antics and giggles, an exuberant mood,
With the flash of their eyes, they spin tales of cheer,
That echo through branches for all of us near.

Beneath the tall ferns, a gathering starts,
With mushrooms as tables and bubbles for arts,
Confetti of petals drifts down from above,
Each drop is a token of friendship and love.

As dawn breaks anew, in a soft golden hue,
The woodland awakens to something so true,
With smiles bursting forth, a jubilant spree,
Creating a world where we're all wild and free.

Echoes of Merriment Under the Canopy

Beneath the leafy crown, we play,
With tickles and jumps, it's a bright day.
Squirrels gossip in a merry tone,
As we giggle softly, never alone.

The sun peeks through, a golden peek,
While we share jokes, it's joy we seek.
Raccoons roll by, they join the jest,
In this wild, funny little fest.

A breeze carries whispers, so sweet and light,
Every twist and turn, leads to delight.
With every chortle, the trees sway low,
Echoes of fun, in the forest's flow.

We dance in circles, shadows sway,
In this leafy haven, let's laugh away.
The world outside can have its gloom,
Here, magic brews, making hearts bloom.

Giggles Amidst the Tall Trees

With every step, the ground is soft,
We leap and bound, our spirits aloft.
A bear prances by with a funny grin,
We hold our bellies, and start to spin.

The birds in chorus, sing silly rhymes,
They tickle our ears, in joyful chimes.
A rabbit hops past, with a jaunty hop,
Its wiggly nose makes our giggles pop.

Tree branches sway like dancers bold,
As we create tales, and laughter unfolds.
Between the trunks, our cheers resound,
In this vibrant space, happiness is found.

With every chuckle, the forest chimes,
Echoes of glee, transcending the times.
Amidst the tall trees, joy takes flight,
In this whimsical breeze under daylight.

Whispers of Joy Beneath the Boughs

Under the boughs, where shadows play,
The giggles and smiles make clouds drift away.
We chase the breeze with our tear-streaked eyes,
As the world around us swells with surprise.

Mushrooms peek out, with a cheeky face,
They share in our fun, a whimsical race.
The ants march in rhythm, a comical line,
Dancing to tunes of the sweetest sign.

Amidst dewdrops, laughter takes flight,
With friends gathered round, everything feels right.
In this corner of peace, where humor espies,
Every thrum of joy leaves a twinkle in the skies.

Beneath the green arch, we make merry sounds,
Painting the air with our joyous rounds.
With hearts intertwined, we cherish the day,
Each moment a spark, in the fun-filled ballet.

Chuckles in the Forest Glade

In the glade where the wildflowers dance,
The breeze tells stories that lead to a prance.
With every tickle of grass on our toes,
We share little secrets that nobody knows.

The sunbeams shimmer like giggles released,
Where bunnies hop high, and the joy is increased.
Each leaf that rustles sings out with glee,
As two happy friends count clouds in a spree.

From shadow to light, we dash in delight,
Chasing the moments that feel oh so right.
With every chuckle, the world seems to shine,
In this pocket of laughter, all troubles decline.

So here in the glade, we let ourselves soar,
With play and with jest, there's always more.
In the laughter we share, there's magic untold,
That sparkles like sunlight on marigold.

Joyful Whispers Among the Pines

In the shade where shadows dance,
The squirrels play a merry prance.
Branches sway, a gentle shake,
Every rustle, a giggling quake.

Sunshine flickers through the leaves,
A chorus of chuckles the forest weaves.
The breeze carries a playful tease,
While nature grins with perfect ease.

Hidden gnomes in mossy boots,
Share silly tales and secret hoots.
The creek hums a bubbly tune,
As frogs croak jokes beneath the moon.

Beneath the boughs, we spin and twirl,
With every whisper, our hearts unfurl.
In this embrace of smiles so wide,
Joy springs forth as our spirits glide.

Echoes of Merriment in the Woods

Bouncing echoes through the trees,
A playground filled with jolly tease.
Chipmunks chirp in playful jest,
As nature's jesters do their best.

In the thickets, secrets shared,
Gentle laughter, none are scared.
A soft breeze leaves us grinning,
With every giggle, a new beginning.

How the colors dance and play,
In sunshine bright, they find their way.
A tickle here, a nudge so sly,
Beneath the branches, joy does fly.

Under the arch of leafy green,
Every moment feels serene.
The woods resound with glee so bright,
Hearts aflutter, pure delight.

Beneath the Canopy of Giggles

Beneath the leaves where shadows gleam,
Whispers weave a shared dream.
Acorns drop, a playful sound,
In this haven, joy is found.

The flowers chuckle with the dawn,
As bees hum tunes, the day is drawn.
Pine cones tumble, a slippery move,
In nature's game, we find our groove.

With every rustling, a smile ignites,
The chitter chats bring pure delights.
Under branches, we laugh and sigh,
With every moment, spirits fly.

Echoes play through the boughs,
Tickling fancies, cheerfulness vows.
In this paradise of joy, we stand,
Forever united, hand in hand.

The Forest's Delightful Serenade

In the heart where whispers twine,
The forest sings a song so fine.
Rustling leaves burst into cheer,
Every chuckle, a song to hear.

Mice in caps parade around,
As woodland laughter wraps the ground.
A fox with pranks and a sheepish grin,
In this playful realm, all win.

Sunlight filters through the trees,
Casting shadows that sway with ease.
As branches wiggle, secrets unfold,
Every giggle a joy untold.

Behold the splendor in nature's arms,
A gathering of wits and charms.
With every echo, our hearts unite,
In the forest's midst, the world feels right.

Echoes of Happiness Among the Evergreens

Beneath the high and swaying trees,
Chirps and giggles swirl like leaves.
Squirrels play tag, a merry chase,
While shadows dance with joyful grace.

In the glen where sunlight beams,
Ducklings waddle, plotting schemes.
Whispers drift on gentle air,
Every sound a happy flair.

A frog jumps high with croaky quips,
While butterflies perform their flips.
Nature's jesters, spry and free,
Unfolding joy for all to see.

With every rustle and each cheer,
Moments spark, like bells they ring clear.
Among the pines, wild and true,
Happiness blooms in every hue.

Harmonizing Grins in Nature's Realm

Twinkling stars through branches peek,
Crickets chirp, their song unique.
A bumblebee hums along the way,
In the twilight, they dance and sway.

Breezes carry chuckles light,
As shadows play in fading light.
The fox strikes poses, quite absurd,
While we watch and hardly stir.

Rusty hinges of a gate,
Swinging laughter, oh what fate!
Hooting owls in cheeky glee,
Boosting spirits by the tree.

In this sanctuary, hearts unwind,
With each giggle, peace we find.
Nature's stage, with joy so grand,
Where every moment's unplanned.

Lighthearted Adventures Among the Boughs

A swing hangs low from a sturdy limb,
Giggles echo, voices brim.
Kids chase shadows, laughter spills,
As pine trees cradle all the thrills.

Marshmallows roast on crackling fire,
Stories shared, never tire.
Mischief reigns as night draws near,
With silly games that spread good cheer.

Jumping squirrels, quirky plays,
In this kingdom, joy stays.
Winding paths lead to delight,
Where dawn breaks with pure insight.

Every thicket whispers fun,
While time dashes like the sun.
Together we'll make silly scenes,
Where nature holds our wildest dreams.

Endless Merriment in the Dappled Shade

In dappled light, the laughter blooms,
Echoing through the quiet rooms.
Tales unfold beneath the trees,
Where every song brings memories.

Chipmunks chatter, brisk and bright,
Glimmers play in fading light.
Tall grasses sway with teasing grace,
While us playfully hide and chase.

The brook giggles past the rocks,
Tickling feet, like dancing clocks.
Sunset paints the skies with cheer,
As friends gather, drawing near.

In this haven, joy's reigns supreme,
Where each heartbeat is a dream.
And through the twilight fading slow,
We share the bliss of nature's show.

Heartfelt Chuckles in the Clearing

In the glade where humor grows,
The squirrels play hide and seek,
Funny faces in the bows,
Nature's giggles, soft yet sleek.

A jolly breeze spills through the trees,
While birds chirp silly songs,
Everyone joins in with ease,
As joy dances, righting wrongs.

Beneath the sun, we share a jest,
With rolling hills as our stage,
Each pun and quip, we're truly blessed,
In this merry woodland page.

Rolling laughter, echoes cheer,
Even shadows can't resist,
Among the pines, we hold so dear,
This place where humor does exist.

The Playful Spirit of the Lodgepole

In the shade of tall timber,
Whispers of fun fill the air,
With nimble feet, we lightly glimmer,
Creating moments, full of flair.

Bouncing squirrels with acorn hats,
Chipmunks dance, one-two-three,
Nature laughs while hearing chats,
In this haven, wild and free.

Frogs leap high with goofy glee,
Round leaves, they hop and skip,
Silly faces them we see,
As friendship takes a playful trip.

Chirping crickets sing along,
The wind plays tricks on the grass,
Here we gather, right or wrong,
In joy's embrace, we always pass.

Joy Unleashed in Nature's Embrace

Among the pines, the spirits soar,
With chuckles rising through the mist,
Every twig and leaf we adore,
Nature's laughter can't be missed.

The brook babbles a witty tune,
As fireflies sparkle in delight,
Together we dance beneath the moon,
Creating tales that feel so right.

Brushing against the playful breeze,
We share our quirks with every sway,
Beneath the bark, the heart just frees,
In this beauty, we laugh and play.

With sunbeams filtering through the trees,
Each smile shared ignites the scene,
In whispers soft, we feel the tease,
Of nature's grace, bright and serene.

Playful Shadows on the Forest Floor

In the twilight, shadows dance,
With giggles bubbling like a stream,
Playful squirrels take a chance,
To steal our hearts in a gleam.

A trickster breeze will pull a hat,
The daisies chuckle at our plight,
As twirling leaves become a mat,
We gather 'round, pure delight.

The melodies of birds entwined,
Echoes of joy, a lively choir,
In the forest, laughter's crafted,
In every moment, we aspire.

With every step, the fun ignites,
As shadows play in evening light,
Here in nature's warm invites,
Our spirits soar, pure and bright.

Frolics by the Foot of the Trees

Squirrels dance and prance with flair,
Chasing tails in the cool, crisp air.
Beneath the shade, they leap and bound,
Creating joy, a playful sound.

Frogs wear crowns of lily pads,
Croaking songs, so spare the fads.
Each jump brings giggles, light and free,
As nature plays its symphony.

A rabbit hops with floppy ears,
Tickling the grass, it brings us cheers.
With every bounce, a chuckle grows,
In this forest where mirth bestows.

Underneath the boughs we play,
In this realm where shadows sway.
With innocence and silly glee,
Life's a circus, wild and free.

The Lightheartedness of the Woodland

In the glen where the wildflowers bloom,
Bees wear sunglasses, while gossip consumes.
A turtle spins tales that boast and brag,
While the wind whispers, collecting a rag.

The woodpecker drums a rhythmic tune,
Squirrels join in like a lively cartoon.
Each branch holds secrets, twinkled wide,
Echoing laughter that cannot hide.

Rabbits play tag with mischievous cheer,
Bounding and leaping, without any fear.
The dappled sunlight dances on the floor,
While every critter implores for more.

In this playful haven, joy takes flight,
The spirit of fun twinkles so bright.
In the heart of the woods, smiles take root,
As giggles unfurl, the world is astute.

Nature's Laughing Heartbeat

Breezes tickle the branches high,
As clouds float lazily in a blue sky.
The rustling leaves join in the jest,
Nature's chorus, always the best.

Sprightly deer prance in a comical way,
Dodging the shadows, they leap and sway.
While chipmunks chat with a cheeky grin,
In this lighthearted world, we all win.

The brook bubbles with giggles so sweet,
Rocks join in, they dance on their feet.
Glancing around, the whole world feels gay,
In this carnival green, we play all day.

Every creature leaves behind a smile,
As we frolic and giggle, mile after mile.
In this woodland paradise, hearts can soar,
With joy in abundance, forevermore.

Vibrations of Joy in the Air

In the canopy high, a jester sings,
Fluffy clouds chase the thrill of wings.
Mice with masks of bright, funky colors,
Paddle about like joyful brothers.

Dancing shadows on a sunlit trail,
The playful breeze tells a whimsical tale.
Each rustle carries whispers of glee,
As berries dangle from branches carefree.

Bouncing bunnies in a frolicking race,
With spirited hops, they conquer space.
Their laughter rings through the vibrant shade,
In this wonderland, all worries fade.

The tickle of grass against tiny toes,
The beats of joy in the heart, it flows.
In this vibrant realm, the spirit ignites,
With cheerful songs that light up our nights.

Chortles Under the Tall Trees

Beneath the pines, a chuckle flows,
Squirrels dance while the humor grows.
A tickle in the crisp, cool air,
Joyful echoes everywhere.

Rabbits giggle, jump and play,
As shadows flicker, dart away.
The brook has banter, bubbling bright,
A playful spirit, pure delight.

Revelry in the Evergreen Glade

In the glade, where stories spin,
The trees wear grins, and fun begins.
Chirping birds set a merry tone,
With every note, we feel at home.

The breeze brings whispers, soft and sweet,
While dancing leaves tap happy feet.
Giggling stars twinkle at night,
In this haven, all feels right.

Harmony of Humor in the Wild

Amidst the woods, laughter takes flight,
Mice tell tales by the firelight.
Branches sway in gleeful cheer,
As nature's laughter draws us near.

Jays jest with silly, vibrant calls,
Creating joy as the evening falls.
With every rustle, a new surprise,
In this realm where merriment lies.

Smile-Filled Breezes Through the Branches

The breeze carries whispers, light and fun,
Bouncing voices, a game begun.
Nuts fall down with a playful thud,
A comedy show in a leaf-strewn flood.

Branches sway, a dancers' waltz,
Nature giggles, never halts.
With echoes that wrap like a warm embrace,
Here in this whimsical, magical place.

Cheer Where the Shadows Play

In the glade where shadows dance,
Critters plot a silly chance.
With a wiggle and a waddle,
They giggle while they dawdle.

Breezes tease the leaves so bright,
As they twirl in pure delight.
Frogs croak jokes in froggy tones,
Echoes bounce like silly stones.

Squirrels scamper, tails held high,
With acorn hats, they swiftly fly.
Chirps and chuffs fill up the air,
Tickling each unwary bear.

Every rustle brings a grin,
Nature's laughter deep within.
In this place where joys collide,
Happiness lives side by side.

Uproar in the Emerald Enclave

Underneath the leafy crown,
Whispers turn to giggles round.
Mice in shoes run to and fro,
While foxes steal the sweetest show.

Laughter echoes 'neath the boughs,
Every critter takes a bow.
From the pond, a turtle jests,
Dropping stones like comic guests.

A rabbit hops with such a flair,
Turns a trick without a care.
Twisting branches laugh along,
Nature's heartbeats sing a song.

In the emerald vibrant glade,
All worries gently fade.
Joy's explosion fills the day,
In this wild and fun ballet.

Heartstrings of Joy in the Wilderness

In the wild, where spirits roam,
Every nook feels like a home.
Bears in hats hold jesters' glee,
Frolicking in harmony.

Crickets play their nightly tune,
While stars flash smiles like a boon.
Owls wink with a knowing stare,
As mischief dances in the air.

Squirrels play at hide-and-seek,
Giggling through the forest peak.
Every trail hides laughter's spark,
Lighting up the twilight dark.

In the wilderness, hearts entwine,
Finding joy in every sign.
A tapestry of mirth is spun,
With every creature, life's a fun.

Merriment Beneath the Canopy's Veil

Underneath the boughs so wide,
Tiny feet dance side by side.
With a hop and playful flair,
Joy erupts here, everywhere.

Owls gossip in the night,
While the fireflies shed their light.
The breeze carries a chuckle bright,
As shadows play in moonlit night.

Beetles roll in silly spins,
Winning hearts, the little wins.
Every flutter, every cheer,
Happiness is always near.

In this lush and vibrant place,
Grins and giggles interlace.
The canopy, a secret stage,
Where laughter blooms at every age.

Whispers of Joy Between the Branches

Under a tree with a crooked grin,
Squirrels debate where the nuts have been.
With chattering cheer, they flit about,
Planning a feast, there's no time for doubt.

The birds join in with a cheerful song,
A raucous chorus that lasts all day long.
Branches sway as if they dance,
Nature's own jester in a merry trance.

The sun peeks through with a wink and a nod,
While shadows play tricks on the dreamy sod.
Beneath this canopy, friendships ignite,
Tickles of joy from morning to night.

A breeze carries tales of silly delight,
Of runaway hats and a kite's crazy flight.
With laughter entwined in the soft, rustling leaves,
Every moment beckons, the heart never grieves.

The Sweet Song of Playful Spirits

In a glen where giggles ring clear and bright,
Fireflies dance in the soft moonlight.
A rabbit in boots hops with such flair,
Chasing shadows, without a care.

Mice in a circle are twirling in glee,
While owls chuckle from the old oak tree.
The wind whispers secrets; the leaves spin around,
Filling the night with a whimsical sound.

Each rustle and chirp in this jovial space,
Brings smiles and honey, happiness in grace.
The stars above join the revelry too,
Shining down on the antics that playfully ensue.

Every heartbeat quickens, every spirit takes flight,
In a world full of wonder, joy feels just right.
Together they frolic, the night wild and free,
Celebrating laughter by the old willow tree.

Mirth Sparkling in the Starlit Glade

Beneath the twinkling of a million lights,
Creatures gather for whimsical nights.
A fox dons a hat, a raccoon a bow,
Preparing for antics that steal the show.

With every tickle of the rustling grass,
Strange tales arise as the shadows pass.
A frog serenades under a glowing moon,
While critters all dream of a grand festoon.

From the depths of the forest, a chuckle will ring,
As fireflies spread out their glimmering bling.
Jokes travel swiftly from ear to eye,
In this magical glade where the spirits fly.

So gather your friends, let your worries depart,
In this delight woven into the heart.
For mirth is the magic that fills every dream,
In the starlit glade, life shines like a beam.

The Gullible Grove of Splendid Grins

In a grove where the sunlight tickles the ground,
Whispers of giggles echo all around.
A turtle claims he once flew with the birds,
While crickets compose songs without any words.

A bear in a tutu takes center stage,
Juggling soft berries, a sight to engage.
The crowd bursts with laughter, their sides feeling tight,
At the charming spectacle on that joyful night.

Each creature a clown in this verdant expanse,
Silly pranks turn simple walks into a dance.
A toad on a unicycle begins to parade,
While the crowd roars with joy, unabashedly swayed.

Beneath leafy rooftops, with smiles so wide,
Adventures unfold, where there's no reason to hide.
In this gullible grove, with its splendid display,
Life's quirkiest moments just thrive every day.

Engagements of Cheer in the Canopy

Under the branches, a giggle escapes,
Squirrels are plotting their silly capes.
A dance with the shadows, they wiggle and spin,
Chasing the echoes of joy from within.

The sunbeams chuckle as they peek through,
Painting the laughter in vibrant hues.
A chorus of crows joins the delightful fray,
Singing of mischief that brightens the day.

With rustling leaves, the whispers agree,
Nature's own humor, wild and free.
In every corner, a tickle to find,
A treasure of giggles the forest entwined.

So gather around, let the mirth ignite,
In the heart of the woods, the spirits take flight.
With every moment, joy finds its way,
In the canopy's arms, we laugh and play.

Joyous Experiences in the Forest

Beneath towering pines, a ruckus is grown,
The chatter of critters, in laughter, they've sewn.
Pine cones are flying, a playful parade,
All revel in jest, the forest's charade.

A fox in a hat, quite dapper and slick,
Tumbles through brush, playing tricks oh so quick.
The bunnies are dancing, in circles they leap,
While owls hoot softly, their humor so deep.

On the edge of a stream, jokes ripple about,
Frogs croak their verses, with a jubilant shout.
While leaves swirl around in a spiraled delight,
Each moment a chance to break up the night.

So let's embrace fun with arms open wide,
In the laughter of woods, where critters abide.
Each tree holds a tale, shared freely and bright,
Underneath the green glow, pure joy takes flight.

Celebrations Beneath the Canopy

In the nooks where the sunlight flickers and beams,
Ants host a party, or so it seems.
With crumbs for a feast and the moss as their ground,
They dance in delight, in rhythm profound.

A bear brings the honey, jars dripping with glee,
While chipmunks parade, so proud and carefree.
The thicket is bustling, alive with delight,
As every small creature joins in for the night.

Jays share their stories, both tall and absurd,
While whispers of laughter are playfully heard.
A raindrop joins in, a sassy surprise,
As moonlight sparkles in shimmery eyes.

So rally the woodland, let's join in the cheer,
With joy all around, there's nothing to fear.
In this gathering grand, where humor holds sway,
Beneath leafy canopies, we frolic and play.

Whirlwinds of Fun in the Leaves

In the swirling leaves, a whirlwind takes flight,
The rustling giggles dance through the night.
With a splash of color, the pumpkins all grin,
Spinning in circles, the chuckles begin.

Twirling around, in a flurry of sights,
Rabbits in costumes, what comical heights!
The shadows are playing, a whimsical game,
Each flicker is teasing, nothing is tame.

A breeze plays a tune on the branches up high,
While crickets tap dance, and fireflies fly.
In this flutter of mirth, the woods come alive,
In the heart of the forest, pure joy will thrive.

So let's twirl together, with hearts ever light,
In these whirlwinds of fun that stretch deep in the night.
For nature's own laughter is waiting to share,
In the beauty of woods, we all feel the flare.

Chimes of Glee in the Wilderness

Beneath the tall trees, we dance and sway,
With giggles that echo, come join the fray.
Squirrels chatter tales, oh what a sight,
While shadows play tricks in the fading light.

Breezes whisper secrets, we can't resist,
In this playful haven, joy coexists.
Frogs leap in rhythm, birds chirp in tune,
As nature composes a whimsical croon.

We toss pine cones, our laughter soars,
Through thickets and glades, where mischief abores.
Each glance a spark, ignites our delight,
In this wild refuge, everything feels right.

So let's spin around 'til our heads are light,
Chasing shadows dancing, into the night.
With every good jest shared among our crew,
The world laughs with us, in a beautiful hue.

Enchanted Moments by the Timberline

In the shade of bold pines, we play and shout,
Crafting our dreams, chasing fears about.
A critter wears goggles, we can't help but snort,
With each odd game, we ignite our sport.

Winks from the chipmunks, their chatter is sweet,
As we run through the ferns, dodging our feet.
The sunbeams tumble, creating a show,
We burst into fits, unable to slow.

The breeze it tickles, like soft little hands,
We gather round barrels, with laughter unplanned.
Kites caught on branches, a humorous sight,
A flock of great giggles, unleashed in the light.

So tell me a story, of fools at their games,
Under the canopy, joy reigns with no shame.
These moments hold magic, it's clear and it's bright,
With spirits like ours, the day feels just right.

Bliss Among the Rooted Sentinels

Amid the tall trunks, we share our glee,
Planting our feet, feeling light as a bee.
A jester joins in, wearing socks on his hands,
As we chuckle together, expanding our bands.

The river sings softly, its playful refrain,
We set sail on leaves, our laughter the chain.
Bubbles of mirth float through branches so wide,
Chasing the sunbeams that giggle and hide.

Sticks become wands, and mud pies appear,
In this realm of jests, there's nothing to fear.
A game of pretend, where all are so spry,
With butterflies joining, they flutter and fly.

So let's spin our stories, the day's nearly done,
As stars blink above, welcoming the fun.
With every shared moment, our spirits take flight,
We treasure this joy, in the hush of the night.

Whimsy Wrapped in Green

Underneath the leafy maze, laughter flows,
We share tales of gremlins, and how mischief grows.
A deer prances by, its dance makes us cheer,
As whispers of whimsy fill all that we hear.

A chorus of giggles, the group starts to sway,
Imagining stories of a frog's grand ballet.
With twigs as our batons, we conduct from afar,
Creating a symphony beneath the bright star.

Our laughter sprouts flowers, wild and so free,
As shadows of moments dance under the tree.
Dust bunnies tumble, our antics they meet,
While nature chuckles gently beneath our feet.

So let's dream as we wander the paths made of fun,
In our enchanted forest, we'll play till we're done.
With friends who bring smiles, and stories to share,
Every leaf carries laughter, lighting the air.

Heartfelt Revelries in the Cleared Space

In the clearing where joy resides,
Frolic and banter cannot hide.
Whispers of giggles, wild and free,
Dance in the air like a honeybee.

Friends gather round, a bright array,
Swapping tall tales in a playful way.
With every chuckle, the sunlight glows,
Beneath the shade where the soft breeze flows.

Mischief sparkles in the sunlit beams,
Tickling fancies, igniting dreams.
Every grin a sweet surprise,
In this haven that never sighs.

So raise a toast to the moments bright,
Fill the clearing with pure delight.
With hearts alight, we forever play,
In this joyful spot, we'll find our way.

Harmony of the Happy Trail

On paths where giggles intertwine,
Every step a playful sign.
Friends skip along, a merry race,
Finding joy in every place.

Tales rise along the winding track,
Echoes of laughter, no looking back.
With every twist, a chuckle unfolds,
In the sun's embrace, warmth it holds.

Stumbling over roots, oh what a sight,
Gleeful antics from morning to night.
Nature chuckles in rustling trees,
As we weave through whispers on the breeze.

Every footprint marks a lighthearted dream,
The happy trail flows like a lively stream.
With joyful hearts and spirits bright,
We dance together in pure delight.

Sprightly Tales Among the Pines

Amidst the pines, where shadows play,
Silly stories brighten the day.
Each branch sways to the giggles' beat,
As friends converge for a fun-filled meet.

With crinkled eyes and joyous grins,
We spin our yarns, where humor begins.
As the sun dips low, we sing our tune,
The moon's soft glow, our playful boon.

Mirth dances high on the pine-scented air,
Leaving behind every worry and care.
For in these woods, we find our cheer,
In the heart of a circle, everything's clear.

So come join the whimsy, an open invite,
To the tales that shimmer under soft twilight.
Among the pines, we find our place,
In a world woven with laughter and grace.

The Festive Calm of the Canopy

Under the canopy, where shadows meet,
A chorus of joy skips to the beat.
With whispers of fun drifting through the leaves,
Inside this haven, the heart believes.

Chiming laughter like distant chimes,
We weave our stories, no need for rhymes.
Every glance a spark, a wink, a cheer,
Filling the air with joy sincere.

Around the trunks, we lose our fears,
Celebrating moments, dismissing tears.
In the gentle sway of the leafy crown,
We find our bliss; let worries drown.

So gather near, where memories flow,
In the festive calm, let happiness grow.
With every chuckle, the forest glows,
As the magic of friendship always shows.

Revelry in the Rustic Shadows

In the whispering woods where we play,
Jokes tumble out like they're on display.
Silly faces and games abound,
Joy bounces back, it knows no bound.

Around the fire, stories ignite,
With each punchline, our spirits take flight.
The night is filled with chuckles and glee,
Under the stars, so wild and free.

The owls look down with a bemused stare,
While we share secrets in the cool night air.
In the flicker of flames, our laughter sways,
Echoing softly, in whimsical ways.

As the moonlight dances on each beaming face,
We're lost in delight, our own sacred space.
With every cheer, we spin and twirl,
In the rustic woods, our hearts unfurl.

Merrymaking Under the Timber

Beneath the branches, we gather tight,
With stories and silliness, pure delight.
Giggles and whispers, the night our friend,
Carving fresh memories that never end.

From the crackling fire, warmth does rise,
With cheeky banter and brightened eyes.
The songs we sing, off-key but bright,
Fill the air with joy, a merry sight.

In this woodland haven, where jokes flow free,
A spontaneous dance, just you and me.
Spinning like tops, in a playful spree,
Under the timber, alive with glee.

As shadows flicker in the dimming light,
We share hearty laughs, oh what a sight!
The trees sway gently to our joyful call,
In the embrace of nature, we find it all.

Euphoria on the Windy Trail

On the winding path where the wildflowers sway,
We find our rhythm, come what may.
Chasing each other, in a playful race,
With laughter that echoes, a raucous embrace.

Up and down hills, we tumble and roll,
Every stumble just adds to the whole.
In the spirit of jest, we bear our hearts,
With every misstep, a fresh work of art.

The breeze carries whispers of fun-filled tales,
As we weave through the woods on our merry trails.
Every corner turned, unveils surprise,
Showing us wonder through each other's eyes.

As dusk settles in, and the stars peek out,
A chorus of chuckles is what it's about.
With eyes full of mirth, we revel in this,
On the windy trail, secures our bliss.

Glee in the Grove of Green

In the grove of green where we frolic and play,
The sun filters through, brightening the day.
With quirky antics and playful pranks,
We dance round and round, giving thanks.

Silly hats made of leaves on our heads,
Giggling at memories that laughter spreads.
Nature's our stage, and we play our part,
With joy rooted deep in each wild heart.

Frogs leap and croak, they join in our fun,
As we prance and play in the warmth of the sun.
The trees sway along to our jubilant cheer,
In the grove of green, there's nothing to fear.

As twilight approaches, painting skies deep,
We promise these moments, our secrets to keep.
In shared gleeful whispers, we let our souls sing,
In the grove of green, we find everything.

The Playful Spirit of the Forest

In the woods where shadows dance,
Squirrels prance in silly chance.
A fox in boots, a bear in ties,
With joyful quips, they catch the eyes.

They twirl and spin, what a sight!
A rabbit's hop, a dragonfly's flight.
With every giggle, every cheer,
The trees seem to smile, drawing near.

A raccoon juggles acorns bright,
While crickets chirp with pure delight.
Amidst the leaves, the laughter rings,
As nature dons her playful wings.

Under the boughs, the fun won't cease,
Where every critter finds their peace.
Join the mirth, just take a peek,
In this forest, it's joy they seek.

Joyful Ramblings in Nature's Arms

Through trails where wildflowers sway,
A chorus sings at the end of the day.
A chipmunk's joke makes the sunbeam glow,
With whispers of breezes, they steal the show.

Mice on scooters, racing so fast,
While owls hoot jokes from the skies vast.
Beneath the branches, smiles abound,
In this vibrant wonderland, joy is found.

A butterfly flutters, a prankster at heart,
Tickling the petals, a delicate art.
As whimsies weave through the vibrant red,
The songbirds know where giggles are fed.

So stroll with glee through this grand display,
Find a sunny patch, come out and play.
Amongst the flowers, hear nature's call,
In these joyful ramblings, we gather all.

The Rustic Revelry of Nature's Hideout

In a glade where pine cones fall,
The critters gather, great and small.
With jesters' caps and playful glee,
They sing and dance, so wild and free.

A porcupine cracks a witty line,
While birds chirp tunes that sparkle and shine.
Tails twirling like ribbons in flight,
The rustling leaves echo sheer delight.

A turtle slips on a banana peel,
While frogs leap high in a funny reel.
Each little joke shared on the breeze,
Turns the moment into memories with ease.

Here in this haven, the sky's so bright,
With laughter ringing through day and night.
Nature's own party, unrestrained,
In rustic revelry, joy's unchained.

Amusement Underneath the Azure Sky

Beneath the azure, life takes flight,
Unfolding scenes of sheer delight.
A squirrel spins tales with mischievous flair,
While grasshoppers dance without a care.

The sunbeams chuckle, the clouds reply,
As critters play tricks with a wink of the eye.
A tortoise crafts bridges with sticks and mud,
In this world of whimsy, joy freely floods.

Parrots throw shade, just out of reach,
As weasels share secrets, the funniest speech.
Creatures unite, a joyous parade,
Under the sky where plans are made.

With heartbeats racing and spirits so bold,
The stories unfold, both new and old.
In this joyous realm, both near and far,
Amusement thrives, like a twinkling star.

Fables of Fun by the Fir

In the shadow of the tree, so grand,
A squirrel danced, a sight so planned.
With acorns flying high in the air,
The giggles echoed, light as a prayer.

A crow cawed loud, a joke to spin,
As rabbits chuckled, their cheeks in a grin.
Each creature knew, the secret they shared,
It's all in the fun, nobody dared.

The fox in his wit, with a wink so sly,
Told tales of mischief, while passersby.
With a hop and a skip, the day flew by,
Underneath branches, they soared through the sky.

A feast was laid out, so silly and bright,
With mushrooms as hats, a comical sight.
In the tales spun here, joy knows no end,
In the heart of the woods, where giggles blend.

Jests among the Whispering Pines

Beneath the pines, the stories blow,
With whispers soft, and laughter low.
A deer would leap with a jolly flair,
While chipmunks scoffed, without a care.

A hedgehog rolled in a playful daze,
As bees buzzed on with their pot of glaze.
Each rustle and chuckle, a riddle so bright,
Spinning merry tales deep into the night.

The nightingale crooned a silly tune,
Where shadows danced 'neath the smiling moon.
Mice held court with their tiny glee,
While owls perched high, watching the spree.

As twilight approached, the fun didn't fade,
From prickly jokes, to pranks that were played.
In a world of whimsy, no sorrow finds space,
Among the pines, everyone knows their place.

A Symphony of Grins in the Glade

In the glade where shadows play,
A band of friends came out to stay.
With tricks and jests that ne'er would tire,
They spun their tales around the fire.

A goat wore glasses, quite absurd,
While frogs chimed in with croaks unheard.
They danced and twirled in a merry spell,
In chorus sweet, they readied to yell.

The bunnies raced with tricks on their feet,
Finding laughter in every heartbeat.
From leaf to leaf, their stories flew,
Each giggle hopeful, and always new.

At dusk, the stars shone bright and bold,
As jokes were spun, and tales retold.
In the heart of the glade, joy would reign,
Among the twinkle of stars, none felt a pain.

Frolics Beneath the Tall Spruces

Beneath the tall ones, so wise and old,
A puppy tumbled, full of gold.
With paws that slipped on dew-kissed grass,
The echoes of laughter would not let pass.

An otter slid by, took a belly flop,
While toads croaked loudly, as if to stop.
The giggles rang from dawn till night,
In this playful heart, all felt light.

A game of tag drew everyone near,
With slides and rolls that brought them cheer.
Squirrels conspired with cunning delight,
Pulling shenanigans under starlit night.

In a world where joy was truly alive,
Each creature's grin, they'd gladly strive.
From dawn till dusk, they'd frolic and play,
Beneath the tall spruces, love lights the way.

A Tapestry of Merriment Among the Pines

Beneath the branches, giggles swell,
Squirrels dance and the sunsets yell.
A whoopee cushion, a prankster's delight,
Echoes of joy fill the cool, crisp night.

Frolicsome whispers through the green,
A game of hide-and-seek, oh so keen.
Raccoons juggle nuts with flair,
Tripping o'er logs without a care.

Moonlight chuckles, shadows play,
As stars join in, they twinkle away.
A chorus of snickers in perfect tune,
Under the watch of a mischievous moon.

Nature's own jesters in perfect sync,
The pine trees nod; there's no time to think.
Each moment crafted in giddy strife,
Crafting a tapestry, woven with life.

Secrets of Joy in the Silent Grove

In a grove where secrets whisper low,
A hidden prankster puts on a show.
A frog croaks loudly, a comical sound,
Discussing the antics all around.

Chipmunks gather for a tea-time treat,
Pass the acorns—oh, what a feat!
Nutty concoctions in leafy bowls,
With laughter bubbling from tiny souls.

Gusts of wind carry tales of delight,
While shadows play tricks until it's night.
The trees giggle, their branches sway,
As light-hearted mischief leads the way.

Joy abounds in this hushed abode,
With friendly banter an easy road.
Under canopies woven with cheer,
The secrets of joy are tucked in here.

Riotous Laughter in the Wilderness

In the wilderness where silliness reigns,
Animals frolic, shedding their chains.
A bear in a tutu does a grand spin,
While chipmunks clap, urging him to win.

Every rustle and giggle ignites,
As critters join in on wild delights.
A rabbit tickles a sleepy old fox,
While owls gather round to trade strange talks.

Goofy antics at the riverbank,
Where fish tell jokes with a cheeky prank.
The laughter cascades like a playful stream,
Echoing far, stirring up a dream.

Beneath the sky, joy spreads like fire,
With wiggles and jiggles, hearts grow higher.
Nature's own revelers in a spree,
Creating a raucous symphony free.

Amusement in the Pine-Needle Carpet

On a carpet of needles, giggles arise,
Where shadows dance and spirit flies.
A woodpecker knocks with a quirky beat,
While rabbits line up for a game so sweet.

An acorn rolls down with a shifty glance,
Inviting the crowd to join the dance.
The forest joins in, steps out of line,
In a playful chaos so purely divine.

Frogs do the hula beneath leafy crowns,
With laughter sweeping through the quaint towns.
A chorus of voices, both young and bold,
Weaving humor into the stories told.

With each new twist, the fun unfolds,
As whimsical patterns of joy take hold.
The pine-needle carpet, a stage so grand,
Where hilarity blossoms, hand in hand.

Radiant Moments in the Forest Fold

In the heart of the green, where the tall trees sway,
A chipmunk danced funny, brightening the day.
With acorns in hand, it jived with delight,
Spinning and twirling, a whimsical sight.

A squirrel on a branch, with a cap full of nuts,
Played peek-a-boo games, evoking light chuckles.
The breeze tickled leaves, with whispers of cheer,
While shadows grew longer, bringing joy near.

Bees buzzed in tune, as they hum nature's song,
While birds joined the chorus, making laughter strong.
The sunlight dripped gold on the forest so bright,
Creating a canvas of joyous delight.

With friends all around and the grass underfoot,
We chased every giggle, as nature took root.
These moments so radiant, so rich and so free,
In the forest's embrace, we're happy as can be.

The Irresistible Allure of Nature's Smile

Beneath the wide sky, where the daisies bloom,
A fox tried to dance, drawing joy from the gloom.
It tumbled and rolled, with a glint in its eye,
A truly sly performer, oh how it could try!

On logs, playful critters, a comedic brigade,
Rehearsed little skits, in the sun-dappled shade.
Each slip and each trip turned to musical fun,
In this vibrant stage, under golden sun.

The wind whispered secrets through branches so tall,
Tickling the cheeks of the creatures so small.
A hare in a hat, yes, a ludicrous sight,
Waving a paw, bidding all a good night.

With roots that embrace in a whimsical way,
The forest called forth, come laugh and to play.
Its smile was infectious, its spirit so bright,
In this wondrous habitat, hearts took their flight.

Stories of Merriment and Mirth

Gathered by the brook, where the ripples sing,
A raccoon told tales of the mischief it brings.
With eyes wide with glee, oh the antics it spun,
Each story a gem, oh the bubbling fun!

A badger joined in, with a laugh from the nook,
Sharing wild pranks that he'd pulled from the book.
The giggles erupted, as time danced away,
In this woodland realm, where bright spirits play.

Fluttering butterflies carried whispers so light,
And the ants marched in rhythm, a zany delight.
With each twist and turn, the laughter would flow,
As friends came together, in the warmth of a glow.

From pine needles soft to the wildflower cheer,
Every moment enchanted felt splendidly clear.
In stories of merriment, bonds grew so tight,
In this grove of joy, every heart felt so light.

Savoring Playfulness in the Pinewood

Through paths lined with pines, where the sunlight bends,

The shadows played tricks, like mischievous friends.
A bear slipped on berries, oh what a surprise,
As we laughed till we cried, under wide-open skies.

The echoes of chuckles danced around the trees,
As squirrels debated the best way to tease.
A pitter-patter of feet, caught in silly split,
Amidst the tall branches, our joy chose to sit.

With the breeze blowing softly and hearts so alive,
In the theater of nature, we truly could thrive.
Every rustle and giggle painted memories bold,
In the warmth of the woods, stories endlessly told.

So here in the pinewood, where spirits ignite,
We savored the playfulness, pure and so bright.
In the depths of the forest, laughter shall soar,
Welcoming magic, and always wanting more.

www.ingramcontent.com/pod-product-compliance
Lightning Source LLC
Chambersburg PA
CBHW072220070526
44585CB00015B/1415